NEURODIVERGENT FRIENDLY SELF-CARE WORKBOOK FOR AUTISTIC ADULTS

UNMASK, EMBRACE YOUR AUTISM DIAGNOSIS AND THRIVE AS YOUR AUTHENTIC SELF

NEURO NURTURE

NORTH STAR PRESS

CONTENTS

Introduction v

1. PHYSICAL AND SENSORY SELF CARE 1
   Sensory Mapping Your Space 1
   Create a Sensory Comfort Zone 3
   Personal Sensory Toolkit Checklist 3

2. EMOTIONAL AND MENTAL SELF CARE 6
   Emotional Awareness and Tracking 6
   Sensory-Friendly Mindfulness Practice 8
   Personal Positive Affirmation Creation 9

3. COGNITIVE AND ROUTINE BASED SELF CARE 13
   Designing a Flexible Routine 13
   Strengthening Executive Functioning 16
   Managing Unexpected Changes 18

4. SOCIAL SELF CARE 20
   Social Cue Observation Practice 20
   Building Your Relationship Blueprint 21
   Practicing Scripts for Social Scenarios 22

5. ENVIRONMENT AND SENSORY SELF CARE 25
   Crafting Your Sensory Haven 25
   Exploring Aromatherapy and Textures 26
   Creating a Nature-Inspired Space 28

6. SELF ADVOCACY AND PROFESSIONAL SELF CARE 31
   Navigating Workplace Politics and Culture 31
   Communication Practice 33
   Networking and Support 35

7. EMBRACING NEURODIVERSITY AND STRENGTHS 38
   Reflection on Masking 38
   Strengths Inventory 41
   Special Interests Mapping 42
   Setting Strength-Based Goals 43
   Visualizing Your Authentic Life 43

Also by Neuro Nurture 49

INTRODUCTION

Imagine a self-care journey crafted specifically for you—one that highlights your unique strengths, celebrates your neurodiversity, and honors your individuality. *Neurodivergent-Friendly Self-Care Workbook for Autistic Adults* is filled with tools and exercises designed to help you prioritize your well-being, deepen your self-awareness, and create a truly authentic life. Whether you're seeking to establish meaningful routines, navigate sensory challenges, or strengthen connections, this workbook is tailored to meet you exactly where you are.

Created as a companion to *Self-Care for Autistic Adults*, this workbook provides hands-on exercises to apply and expand upon the insights shared in the main book. However, it also stands alone as a powerful resource, offering practical strategies and thoughtful reflections for anyone looking to embrace self-care and authenticity in their daily life.

How to Use This Workbook

- **Choose Your Path:** Use this workbook alongside *Self-Care for Autistic Adults* to enhance your learning, or dive into it on its own for practical, hands-on self-care strategies.
- **Go at Your Own Pace:** Take your time with each chapter and exercise. This workbook is designed to meet you where you are and adapt to your needs.
- **Engage with the Exercises:** Write, draw, or brainstorm directly in the workbook. The activities are here to guide your self-discovery and help you apply concepts to your daily life.
- **Personalize Your Experience:** Every individual's self-care journey is unique. Focus on the exercises that resonate with you and revisit sections as often as needed.

Introduction

This workbook is your companion in creating a life that celebrates your strengths and supports your well-being. Let it guide you as you embrace your authentic self and design a self-care routine that feels right. To help you meditate, unwind, and embrace the themes of each chapter, we've included a unique coloring image at the end of every section. Let's get started!

1. PHYSICAL AND SENSORY SELF CARE

The first step toward effective self-care is understanding how your physical environment and sensory experiences impact your well-being. This chapter explores how to design spaces and routines that promote sensory ease and comfort tailored to your unique needs. By paying attention to lighting, textures, organization, and sensory tools, you can create a personalized environment that reduces stress and enhances relaxation. Let's explore how you can apply these principles in your daily life with practical exercises that will empower you to take control of your surroundings and make them work for you.

Sensory Mapping Your Space

Objective: Identify elements in your living space that either soothe or overwhelm your senses.

Instructions:

1. Choose one room in your home to focus on. Start with the room you spend most of your time in.
2. Observe the sensory inputs in the room (e.g., lighting, noise, textures, colors, smells).
3. Use the table below to list these inputs and categorize them as calming or overstimulating.
4. Reflect on how these factors affect your mood and note two changes you can make.

Sensory Input	Calming or Stimulating?	Why?
Example: Bright light overhead	Overstimulating	Too harsh, causes eyes to strain

Reflection Prompt:

How does this space currently support or hinder your relaxation? What small changes could make the biggest difference?

_____

_____

_____

_____

_____

Changes I Plan to Make:

1.

_____

2.

_____

3.

_____

Physical and Sensory Self Care

Create a Sensory Comfort Zone

Objective: Design a specific area in your home where you can retreat to decompress.

Instructions:

1. Choose a quiet corner or space.
2. Add at least three sensory-friendly items, like a soft blanket or calming lamp.
3. Customize the space with calming colors and remove clutter.

Describe Your Comfort Zone:

Where is this space located? What items did you include, and why?

_____

_____

_____

Reflection Prompt:

How does this space make you feel? What other changes could improve it?

_____

_____

_____

Personal Sensory Toolkit Checklist

Objective: Build a toolkit to address your sensory needs at home and on the go.

Instructions:

1. Fill out the sensory checklist below to identify comforting textures, sounds, smells, etc.
2. Brainstorm items you already have, could easily purchase, or could make yourself.

3. If you don't have an item yet, write down an alternative you can explore (e.g., use a towel instead of a weighted blanket, or create a calming playlist instead of buying a white noise machine).
4. Reflect on how and when you'll use these items.

Sensory Category	Soothing Preferences	Example Item
Touch (Example)	Soft Textures	Plush Blanket
Touch		
Sound		
Smell		
Visual		
Taste		

How I'll Use My Toolkit:

Write a short plan for how and when you will use your toolkit.

_____

_____

Reflection Prompt:

How will these items help you manage sensory stress or feel more comfortable? What's one item you're most excited to try, and why?

_____

_____

Physical and Sensory Self Care

As we conclude this section on physical and sensory self-care, remember that creating a space tailored to your unique sensory needs can profoundly impact your daily well-being. By addressing the elements of your environment—lighting, textures, colors, and organization—you take an active step toward a more comfortable and peaceful life. Take a moment to unwind with the included coloring page, featuring a soothing, sensory-friendly design, before transitioning to the next chapter, where we'll delve into emotional and mental self-care strategies.

2. EMOTIONAL AND MENTAL SELF CARE

Emotional and mental self-care are essential components of overall well-being, especially for Autistic adults who navigate unique challenges like sensory overload and emotional dysregulation. This chapter explores practical strategies to understand and manage emotions, build resilience, and create moments of calm amidst life's complexities. Through reflection, mindfulness practices, grounding techniques, and positive affirmations, you'll develop tools to better navigate emotional challenges and create a more balanced, fulfilling life.

Emotional Awareness and Tracking

Objective: Recognize patterns in emotional experiences to better understand triggers and responses.

Instructions:

1. For the next three days, set aside 5–10 minutes each evening to reflect on your emotions. Alternatively, you can extend this exercise over a longer period or choose specific days within the next week when you felt particularly overwhelmed. This flexibility allows you to tailor the practice to your unique experiences and schedule.
2. Use the prompts below to guide your reflections and record your answers in the spaces provided.
3. At the end of the week, review your notes to identify patterns and insights.

Emotional and Mental Self Care

Day 1

What were three emotions I experienced most strongly today?

___

What situations or events triggered these emotions?

___

How did I respond to these emotions? Was my response helpful or unhelpful?

___

What is one thing I could try next time to manage these emotions better?

___

Day 2

What were three emotions I experienced most strongly today?

___

What situations or events triggered these emotions?

___

How did I respond to these emotions? Was my response helpful or unhelpful?

___

What is one thing I could try next time to manage these emotions better?

___

Day 3

What were three emotions I experienced most strongly today?

___

What situations or events triggered these emotions?

___

How did I respond to these emotions? Was my response helpful or unhelpful?

___

. . .

What is one thing I could try next time to manage these emotions better?

Reflection Prompt:

What patterns did I notice in my emotional experiences and triggers?

What strategies worked best for managing my emotions? How can I use what I've learned to build better emotional awareness and resilience?

Sensory-Friendly Mindfulness Practice

Objective: Create a daily mindfulness routine tailored to your sensory preferences.

Instructions:

1. Choose a mindfulness activity that aligns with your sensory preferences. Here are some examples:
    - **Grounding with Textures:** Select an object with a soothing texture, like a soft blanket, a smooth stone, or a plush toy. Hold the object in your hands and focus on its texture—run your fingers over its surface, noting how it feels (e.g., soft, warm, rough, or cool).
    - **Grounding with Sound:** Listen to calming music, nature sounds, or white noise. Pay attention to the rhythm, tones, or patterns.
    - **Grounding with Scent:** Use a favorite essential oil (like lavender or chamomile) or a scented candle. Close your eyes, inhale deeply, and focus on the aroma.

2. Practice your chosen mindfulness activity for 5–10 minutes daily. If you're unsure which activity suits you, try a different one each day to see what feels most calming.
3. After practicing, take a few moments to reflect on how the activity influenced your mood and sensory experience:
    - Which grounding technique did you choose, and how did it make you feel?
    - What changes, if any, did you notice in your emotions or physical sensations during or after the practice?
    - Do you feel this technique is something you'd like to continue using? If not, what other technique might you explore instead?

Reflection Prompt:

Over the past week, which mindfulness activity felt most effective for you?

_____

_____

Were there any activities that didn't resonate with you? If so, why?

_____

_____

How did practicing mindfulness impact your emotions and ability to manage sensory input?

_____

_____

What changes, if any, would you make to your mindfulness routine moving forward?

_____

_____

Personal Positive Affirmation Creation

Objective: Develop affirmations to support emotional resilience and positivity.

1. Reflect on the challenges you face and the strengths you wish to nurture. Use the prompts below to guide your thoughts.

2. Write three affirmations that resonate with your goals (e.g., *"I honor my sensory needs,"* or *"I am patient with myself and my growth"*).
3. Place these affirmations somewhere visible, and repeat them daily for a week.
4. After the week, reflect on how this practice influenced your mindset and emotional well-being.
5. Use the tips provided to continue this practice as an ongoing part of your self-care routine

Step 1: Identify Challenges and Strengths

What challenges are you currently facing?

_____

_____

What strengths do you want to build or celebrate?

_____

_____

Step 2: Write Your Affirmations

Write three affirmations based on your reflections. These can be short, empowering statements that support your goals and emotional growth.

1

_____

2

_____

3

_____

Step 3: Weekly Reflection

How did repeating these affirmations affect your mindset or emotions over the past week?

_____

_____

Did any of the affirmations resonate particularly strongly with you? Why?

_____

Would you like to create additional affirmations or adjust the ones you wrote?

Sustaining the Practice

Affirmations work best when they become a regular part of your routine. Here are some tips to help you continue this practice:

1. **Create a Rotation of Affirmations:**
   - Every Sunday, take a few minutes to review your affirmations.
   - Keep the ones that feel meaningful and adjust or add new ones based on your current challenges and goals.
2. **Incorporate Affirmations into Your Daily Routine:**
   - Start your day by reciting an affirmation while brushing your teeth or getting ready.
   - Write an affirmation on a sticky note and place it somewhere visible, like your desk or bathroom mirror.
   - Use affirmations as part of a mindfulness practice by pairing them with deep breathing or grounding techniques.
3. **Reflect Weekly:**
   - Dedicate time at the end of each week to journal about how the affirmations have impacted your mood, mindset, or daily life.
   - Use prompts like:
     - *Which affirmation resonated most with me this week?*
     - *What new affirmation could I create to address current challenges?*
4. **Celebrate Progress:**
   - Acknowledge the changes you notice over time.
   - Even small shifts in your mindset or behavior are worth celebrating as signs of growth.

Ongoing Reflection Prompts:

How do my affirmations support my emotional well-being and resilience?

What new affirmations can I create to address changes in my life or challenges I'm facing?
___
___

As we wrap up this chapter on emotional and mental self-care, remember that nurturing your emotional well-being is a journey of self-awareness, mindfulness, and resilience. By exploring grounding techniques, creating affirmations, and understanding your emotional patterns, you take important steps toward building balance and calm in your life. To reflect and unwind, enjoy the included coloring page as a mindful activity before moving forward on your self-care journey.

3. COGNITIVE AND ROUTINE BASED SELF CARE

Building routines and enhancing cognitive skills are powerful ways to create stability and clarity in your daily life. For Autistic adults, establishing a balance between structure and flexibility can reduce anxiety and foster a sense of control, while cognitive strategies can improve focus and executive functioning. This chapter explores how to create adaptable routines, sharpen mental tools, and embrace productivity systems tailored to your unique needs. By integrating these strategies, you can empower yourself to navigate your day with greater confidence and ease.

Designing a Flexible Routine

Objective: Create a personalized routine that balances structure with flexibility.

Instructions:

1. Identify Key Activities: List the essential tasks you need to complete this week. You can group them by priority or category (e.g., work, self-care, household).

Task / Activity	Priority (High/Medium/Low)

2. Plan Buffer Times: Add 10–15 minute breaks between tasks to allow for transitions or unexpected changes.

Example:

- Task 1: Morning walk (9:00–9:30 AM)

- Buffer: Relax with tea (9:30–9:45 AM)

- Task 2: Start work (9:45 AM)

Write down one or two areas where buffer times could help reduce stress:

_____

_____

_____

3. Add Time for Spontaneity: Schedule moments for relaxation or creative activities. Use this space to brainstorm ideas:

Task / Activity	Time Slot

4. Choose Your Planning Tools:

Decide which tool you'll use to track your routine:

○ Digital planner (e.g., app or calendar)

○ Visual schedule/chart

○ Paper planner or notebook

5. Write your choice and why it works best for you:

_____

_____

_____

5. Review and Adjust:

At the end of the week, reflect on your routine: What worked well?

_____

_____

_____

What would you like to improve for next week?

_____

_____

_____

Strengthening Executive Functioning

Objective: Develop skills to enhance planning, focus, and task management.

Instructions:

1. Choose a Task: Think of a task or project you often struggle with or feel overwhelmed by. It could be something like cleaning a room, preparing a meal, completing a work assignment, or managing an appointment.

---

2. Break the Task into Smaller Steps: Divide the task into small, actionable steps that feel manageable.

For example, you can break down a task such as 'Clean the bedroom' into:

- Step 1: Gather laundry.
- Step 2: Put away items on the floor.
- Step 3: Dust furniture.
- Step 4: Vacuum the carpet.

Write your steps below:

Step 1:

Step 2:

Step 3:

Step 4:

---

3. Set a Clear Goal for the Task:

Define what success looks like for this task. Be specific about the outcome and timeline. For example: *"I will clean the bedroom by Friday evening, focusing on removing clutter and making the space neat."*

_____

_____

_____

4. Reflect on the Experience:

After completing the task, reflect on how breaking it into smaller steps and setting a clear goal helped:

Did breaking the task into steps make it easier to approach? Why or why not?

_____

_____

_____

What would you do differently next time?

_____

_____

_____

Managing Unexpected Changes

Objective: Prepare strategies to handle disruptions with confidence.

Instructions:

Identify three situations where unexpected changes might occur (e.g., canceled plans, a sudden work task).

1. _____

2. _____

3. _____

Develop a contingency plan for each scenario. Include calming techniques or alternative options.

1. _____

2. _____

3. _____

Reflect on how preparing for changes helps reduce anxiety and improve adaptability:

_____
_____
_____
_____

Cognitive and Routine Based Self Care

As we conclude this chapter on cognitive and routine-based self-care, remember that creating structure and enhancing cognitive tools are powerful steps toward greater stability and confidence. By designing flexible routines, strengthening executive functioning, and preparing for unexpected changes, you can navigate daily life with more ease and focus. Incorporating time management strategies and cognitive exercises supports not only your productivity but also your mental clarity and well-being. Take a moment to reflect on these practices, and enjoy the included coloring page as a calming way to visualize and embrace the concepts discussed.

4. SOCIAL SELF CARE

Social self-care involves building meaningful relationships, understanding social dynamics, and finding comfort in social settings. For Autistic adults, navigating social interactions can feel overwhelming, yet with the right tools and strategies, it's possible to create supportive connections and enhance your confidence. This chapter focuses on decoding social cues, managing conversations, building relationships, and thriving in both in-person and online communities. By embracing these approaches, you can foster relationships that are enriching, respectful, and aligned with your values.

Social Cue Observation Practice

Objective: Improve your ability to recognize and interpret social cues in a safe and controlled setting.

Instructions:

1. **Choose a Setting:** Pick a quiet, low-pressure environment to observe social interactions, such as a café, park, or watching a movie.
2. **Observe Non-verbal Cues:** Pay attention to facial expressions, gestures, tone of voice, and body language. Take notes on what you notice, such as a smile indicating friendliness or crossed arms showing discomfort.

Observed Non-verbal Cue	What It Might Mean

Reflect on Alignment: Think about how these cues add meaning to spoken words. Did you notice anything surprising? Write your reflections here:

_____

_____

_____

Building Your Relationship Blueprint

Objective: Define what you value in relationships and create a plan for meaningful connections.

Instructions:

1. **Identify Values:** Write down three qualities that matter most to you in relationships (e.g., honesty, support, shared interests):

_____

_____

_____

2. **Set Boundaries:** Consider what boundaries are essential for your emotional and social well-being (e.g., time alone, limits on physical contact):

_____

_____

_____

3. Find Shared Interests: List activities or hobbies you enjoy that could lead to connections (e.g., book clubs, gaming groups):

_____

_____

_____

4. Plan an Interaction: Think of one way you could meet someone new or connect with an existing friend (e.g., joining a club or scheduling a coffee chat):

_____

_____

_____

Practicing Scripts for Social Scenarios

Objective: Build confidence in navigating common social interactions using prepared language.

Instructions:

1. Choose a Scenario: Choose a situation that feels challenging or happens often, such as introducing yourself, making small talk, or setting a boundary. Write it down here:

_____

_____

2. Practice a Script: Think of a natural, easy-to-remember way to express yourself in this situation. Keep it simple and true to your communication style.

Example Scenarios and Scripts:

- **Introducing Yourself:** "Hi, I'm [Your Name]. I'm really into [hobby/interest]. What about you?"
- **Setting a Boundary:** "I appreciate the invite, but I need some time to recharge. Maybe another time?"

- **Ending a Conversation:** "It's been great talking with you. I need to step away for a bit, but I hope we can chat again soon."

Write your script here:

_____

_____

_____

3. Practice Your Script: Say it out loud a few times in front of a mirror, with a trusted friend, or even to yourself. Notice if it feels natural and adjust if needed.

4. Make It Your Own: After practicing, tweak the script to sound more like how you naturally speak or feel most comfortable. Write your final version here:

_____

_____

_____

Reflect on the Experience:

Did practicing make you feel more prepared or confident? Why or why not?

_____

_____

_____

What other situations could you create scripts for?

_____

_____

_____

Social self-care is about building meaningful connections, navigating social dynamics, and finding comfort in interactions. By understanding social cues, setting boundaries, practicing communication, and nurturing relationships, you can create supportive and enriching social experiences. Whether online or in person, prioritizing connections that align with your values fosters a sense of belonging and emotional well-being. Take a moment to enjoy the included coloring page, reflecting the warmth and comfort of relaxed conversations, as a mindful way to embrace the themes of this chapter.

5. ENVIRONMENT AND SENSORY SELF CARE

Our environment has a profound impact on how we feel and function. For Autistic adults, sensory-sensitive spaces are not just about comfort—they're essential for emotional balance and well-being. From creating calm lighting and soundscapes to incorporating soothing textures and natural elements, this chapter explores practical ways to shape your surroundings into a sensory sanctuary. Whether it's your home, workplace, or even a travel destination, these strategies will empower you to craft spaces that nurture and support your sensory needs.

Crafting Your Sensory Haven

Objective: Identify and adjust sensory triggers in your living space to create a calming environment.

Instructions:

1. Assess Your Space: Spend 5–10 minutes in each room, noting any sensory discomforts like harsh lighting, loud noises, or clutter. Write them down:

_____

_____

_____

. . .

2. Decide on Adjustments: Based on your observations, think about potential changes you could make to enhance comfort. Consider adjustments to::

- **Lighting** (e.g., softer bulbs, dimmable lamps)
- **Sound** (e.g., adding sound-absorbing materials, using a white noise machine)
- **Clutter** (e.g., organizing or decluttering spaces)

List three specific adjustments you plan to make:

_____

_____

_____

4. Reflect on the Changes: After making adjustments, describe how they impacted your mood or comfort:

_____

_____

_____

_____

Exploring Aromatherapy and Textures

Objective: Discover calming scents and soothing textures to create a sensory experience that feels supportive and enjoyable.

Instructions:

1. Start with Scents:

- Visit a local store where you can test essential oils or scented candles (e.g., health food stores, craft stores, or budget-friendly retailers). Many shops have testers available.
- Choose calming scents such as lavender, chamomile, or sandalwood for relaxation, or energizing options like citrus or peppermint for focus.

2. Write down your top three scents and where you found them:

_____

_____

_____

Budget Tip: If purchasing essential oils, consider buying trial-size bottles to experiment before committing to larger quantities. Some online stores offer sample packs of popular scents.

3. Explore Textures:

- Visit a home goods or fabric store where you can touch different materials. Focus on items like plush blankets, smooth fabrics, or textured pillows. Think about what feels soothing or grounding to you.
- If going out isn't practical, explore the items you already have at home. Look for soft clothing, textured rugs, or cozy throws.

Describe three textures you find comforting and where you might use them (e.g., on your couch, bed, or workspace):

_____

_____

_____

4. Combine for a Multi-Sensory Experience: Pair a chosen scent with a favorite texture for a multi-sensory relaxation experience. For example, spray a lavender mist on a soft blanket or place a scented sachet on your bed.

Describe your chosen combination and how it made you feel:

_____

_____

_____

Creating a Nature-Inspired Space

Objective: Bring the calming and grounding elements of nature into your living space in simple and accessible ways.

Instructions:

1. Add Plants to Your Space:

- Start small! Visit a local garden center, grocery store, or even a plant swap group to pick out beginner-friendly plants like succulents, pothos, or spider plants. These are easy to care for and affordable.
- If you're unsure about plant care, ask for advice at the store or search for beginner plant-care tips online.

Write down the plants you've chosen and where you plan to place them in your home (e.g., your desk, window sill, or bedside):

_____

_____

_____

2. Incorporate Natural Materials:

- Look for items made of wood, stone, or other natural materials. For example, a small wooden bowl for your desk, a stone coaster, or a woven basket can add a touch of nature to your room.
- Visit thrift stores, craft markets, or budget-friendly retailers to find affordable natural decor.

Describe two natural materials you've added to your space and how they make you feel:

_____

_____

_____

3. Spend Time in Nature and Reflect:

- Take a short walk in a park, garden, or any nearby green space. Notice the colors, textures, and sounds around you. Collect small items like a leaf, pinecone, or pebble as a reminder of your time outdoors.
- Use these moments to recharge and connect with nature.

What did you observe and feel during your time in nature? Write about any sensory details that stood out to you:

_____

_____

_____

4. Create a Portable Nature Kit: Fill a small box or bag with natural items that bring you joy or calm, such as shells, stones, or dried flowers. Use this kit whenever you need a moment of grounding or comfort.

Create a Portable Nature Kit:

• Fill a small box or bag with natural items that bring you joy or calm, such as shells, stones, or dried flowers. Use this kit whenever you need a moment of grounding or comfort.

List the items you've chosen for your portable nature kit and why you selected them:

_____

_____

_____

Your environment is more than a physical space; it's a reflection of your sensory needs and emotional well-being. By making thoughtful adjustments to lighting, sound, textures, and natural elements, you can create spaces that soothe and support you. Take time to experiment with these strategies and enjoy the process of designing a sensory sanctuary tailored to your unique preferences. As you move forward, remember that even small changes can have a profound impact, turning any space into a haven of comfort and calm.

6. SELF ADVOCACY AND PROFESSIONAL SELF CARE

Imagine walking into your workplace feeling empowered, knowing that your environment supports your unique needs and strengths. For many Autistic adults, navigating professional spaces can feel daunting, but self-advocacy is a tool that can help you shape your work environment into one that works for you. This chapter provides practical steps and strategies for understanding your rights, communicating effectively, navigating workplace culture, and balancing independence with support. Self-advocacy isn't about confrontation—it's about collaboration, creating a professional life that respects and celebrates who you are.

Navigating Workplace Politics and Culture

Objective: To develop an understanding of your workplace culture, build meaningful relationships, and create a plan to navigate workplace dynamics effectively and confidently.

Workplace culture often feels like an unspoken rulebook. Learning to read this "rulebook" can make your professional environment more manageable and empowering. This exercise helps you reflect on your current workplace culture, identify key players, and plan steps to navigate office politics and build positive relationships that align with your goals.

Use the prompts below to explore your workplace dynamics. Take your time to answer honestly and reflect on your observations:

1. Describe your workplace culture (e.g., Is it formal or relaxed? Collaborative or individual-focused?)

2. Who are the key influencers or decision-makers in your workplace? (Consider managers, team leads, or respected colleagues.)

3. What are some behaviors you've observed that are valued in your workplace? (e.g., punctuality, teamwork, taking initiative.)

4. How do you currently participate in your workplace culture? (What roles or activities do you take on? How do you engage with colleagues?)

5. What steps can you take to build positive relationships at work? (Think about how you can connect with others in ways that feel natural and meaningful.)

6. How will you avoid common pitfalls? (e.g., staying away from gossip, maintaining professional boundaries, focusing on constructive feedback.)

Plan of Action

Now, write down one specific action step you will take to better navigate workplace politics or culture. Choose something manageable and meaningful to you:

_____
_____
_____

Reflection and Follow-Up

How will this step help you feel more confident in your workplace?

_____
_____
_____

What support or resources do you need to take this step effectively?

_____
_____
_____

By reflecting on your workplace environment and planning intentional actions, you can build a stronger sense of belonging and agency in your professional life. Navigating workplace politics doesn't mean changing who you are—it's about finding ways to thrive within your environment while staying true to your values and goals.

Communication Practice

Advocating for your needs effectively begins with clear and confident communication. Using a structured template ensures your message is concise and easy to understand. Below is a template you can use and customize for any workplace request.

Template: Clear Need, Reason, Proposed Solution

1. **Clear Need:** Briefly state what you need.
   - Example *"I need a quieter workspace to focus effectively."*

2. **Reason:** Explain why this need is important, focusing on how it affects your work.
   - Example *"The open office environment increases distractions, which makes it difficult to complete tasks efficiently."*
3. **Proposed Solution:** Offer a realistic and cooperative solution.
   - Example *"Could I move to a quieter section of the office or use noise-canceling headphones during focused tasks?"*

1. Write Your Request: Write your own request draft using the template below. Take your time to think about a specific workplace need and how you can present it.

Clear Need:

_____

_____

Reason:

_____

_____

Proposed Solution:

_____

_____

2. Rehearse Your Request: Practice delivering it in front of a mirror or with a supportive friend. Focus on clarity and confidence.

3. Reflect and Adjust: After rehearsing, consider the following questions:

○ Did your message feel clear and direct?

○ Are there any parts you'd like to revise for better flow or tone?

4. Refine Your Request: Make any necessary adjustments and prepare to use it in a real conversation.

_____

_____

_____

Reflection Prompt

How did practicing with the template help you clarify your thoughts?

What additional steps can you take to feel more confident in advocating for your needs?

_____

_____

_____

Networking and Support

Networking doesn't have to mean attending large, overstimulating events or forcing small talk. It's about creating genuine, mutually supportive relationships that align with your goals and values. This exercise will guide you in identifying opportunities, preparing for conversations, and reflecting on the process in a way that feels accessible and supportive of your needs.**Objective:** To build a professional network that feels authentic, manageable, and aligned with your interests, providing you with meaningful connections and a foundation of support.

1. Identify Networking Opportunities

What groups, events, or platforms can you use to connect with like-minded professionals? List at least three possibilities:

1

_____

2

_____

3

_____

2. Prepare Networking Scripts

Craft responses for common networking situations to help you feel confident and prepared. Use the prompts below to create your scripts:

Introducing Yourself:

"Hi, I'm [Your Name]. I work in [Your Field/Role], and I'm really interested in [specific topic]. What about you?"

Starting a Conversation:

"What do you enjoy most about your work in [field/company]?"

Requesting Advice or Resources:

"I'm exploring ways to [goal, e.g., improve a skill, learn more about a topic]. Do you have any advice or resources you'd recommend?"

3. Practice and Reflect

Try out these scripts in a safe setting, such as with a friend or during a small event. Networking should feel like a natural extension of your interests, not a forced activity. As you complete this exercise, focus on creating authentic connections in environments that support your sensory and emotional needs. Let networking be something that enhances your confidence and opens doors to new opportunities. Reflect on your experience:

What felt easy or enjoyable about the interaction?

What would you change or improve for next time?

4. Follow Up: Write a draft follow-up message to someone you connected with:

Self Advocacy and Professional Self Care

Self-advocacy is both a skill and a journey, empowering you to navigate professional spaces with confidence and authenticity. By understanding your rights, communicating effectively, and cultivating a sensory-friendly environment, you can create a workplace that supports your success. Networking and collaboration further reinforce this foundation, providing opportunities for growth and connection. Remember, balancing independence with support is not a limitation—it's a strength that allows you to thrive while fostering inclusivity and understanding in your professional life.

7. EMBRACING NEURODIVERSITY AND STRENGTHS

Imagine a world where every unique mind is not only accepted but celebrated for its distinct perspective. This is the essence of neurodiversity—a concept that views diverse neurological profiles as natural variations in the human experience, rather than deficits or disorders. Embracing neurodiversity means shifting the focus from challenges to strengths, recognizing the unique contributions each individual can make. Whether it's through leveraging personal strengths, channeling the power of special interests, or reframing challenges as opportunities, this chapter invites you to explore the transformative potential of living authentically. Together, we'll uncover strategies to embrace your true self, honor your individuality, and create a life rooted in confidence, creativity, and joy.

Neurodiversity celebrates diverse neurological profiles as natural variations, not deficits. Yet, many Autistic individuals engage in "masking" to conform to societal expectations. While masking can feel necessary, it often comes at the cost of authenticity and well-being. Unmasking is the process of peeling back layers of imposed behaviors to embrace and live as your authentic self.

Reflection on Masking

Objective: To identify instances of masking in your life and reflect on how it has impacted your authenticity and well-being.

Instructions: Let's explore masking in a way that combines reflection and creativity. Whether you're in the process of unmasking or have already embraced your authentic self, this exercise will guide you through a creative and reflective journey. Use the prompts below to explore your relationship with masking and authenticity.

Imagine that masking is like wearing a costume. Take a moment to visualize the mask you wear in situations where you feel you cannot be yourself.

1. Describe your mask: What does it look like? What traits or behaviors does it represent (e.g., traits you felt you needed to hide or behaviors you adopted to fit in.)?

_____
_____
_____

2. How does wearing this mask feel? Does it make you feel safe, exhausted, hidden, or something else?

_____
_____
_____

Now, imagine taking off the mask in a safe space where you can fully be yourself.

3. Who are you underneath the mask? What traits or behaviors emerge when you can fully be yourself?

_____
_____
_____

4. How would unmasking change your interactions or experiences in this scenario? Alternatively, how has unmasking positively impacted your life?

_____
_____
_____

5. Celebrate the unique strengths and qualities that define your unmasked self. What is one strength or quality that shines brightest when you live authentically?

_____
_____
_____

6. How can you use this strength to enhance your daily life or support your goals?

_____

_____

_____

Optional Creative Prompt:

Draw or sketch your mask and your unmasked self in the space below. Use colors, symbols, or shapes to represent the differences.

Strengths Inventory

Objective: To identify personal strengths and explore how they align with both masking and authentic living.

Instructions: Fill in the table below to reflect on how your strengths manifest differently when masking versus when living authentically.

Strength	How It Shows When Masking	How It Shows When Authentic
Example: Creativity	Suppressed to appear "practical"	Thrives in brainstorming sessions

Reflection Prompt:

How can you embrace one of these strengths more fully in your daily life? Write your thoughts below:

_____

_____

_____

Special Interests Mapping

Objective: To explore how special interests can enhance your personal and professional growth.

Instructions: Complete the table below, identifying barriers to engaging with your special interests and steps to overcome them.

Special Interest	Current Engagement Level	Barriers to Full Engagement	Steps to Overcome Barriers

Reflection Prompt:

Choose one special interest. What small action can you take this week to engage with it more fully?

_____

_____

_____

_____

_____

Setting Strength-Based Goals

Objective: To create actionable goals that align with your strengths and support unmasking.

Instructions: Complete the following goal-setting prompts:

1. My strength is:

   _____

2. I want to use this strength to:

   _____

3. The first step I'll take is:

   _____

4. I'll celebrate progress by:

   _____

Visualizing Your Authentic Life

Objective: To visualize and celebrate your journey toward authenticity, highlighting your strengths, passions, and the life you want to live.

Instructions: A vision board is a visual representation of your goals, values, and dreams. It serves as a daily reminder to embrace your authentic self and live in alignment with your true identity. Follow these steps to create your personalized vision board:

1. **Gather Your Materials:**
   - Use a physical board (like corkboard or poster board) or a digital platform (like Pinterest or Canva).
   - Collect magazines, photos, printouts, stickers, or anything visually inspiring.
2. **Reflect on Your Authentic Self:**
   - Think about the life you want to create now that you are unmasking or living authentically. Ask yourself:
     - What brings you joy?
     - What are your passions or special interests?

- What strengths do you want to highlight?
3. **Choose Meaningful Images and Words:**
   - Look for pictures, quotes, or symbols that represent your goals, values, and authentic life.
   - For example, a photo of a serene nature scene could symbolize self-care, while a vibrant color palette might represent creativity.
4. **Arrange and Create:**
   - Place your materials on the board in a way that feels inspiring and cohesive. Don't worry about making it perfect; focus on what resonates with you.
   - Add personal touches like drawings, affirmations, or your favorite colors.
5. **Display Your Vision Board:**
   - Put your board in a space where you will see it regularly, like your bedroom, workspace, or a digital device background.
6. **Engage with Your Vision Board:**
   - Take a moment each day to look at your board and reflect on how you can take small steps toward the life it represents.

Embracing neurodiversity and living authentically is an ongoing journey of discovery, growth, and celebration. As you reflect on the mask you once wore and the strengths that define your unmasked self, know that you are creating a life rooted in alignment with your true identity. If you're still wearing a mask, remember that this does not diminish your worth or the incredible strengths that lie beneath. Unmasking is a deeply personal process that requires courage, patience, and self-compassion.

Your vision board is more than a collection of images; it's a tangible reminder of your commitment to authenticity and the beauty of your neurodiverse mind. Let it inspire you to take steps, big or small, toward a life where your strengths and passions shine unapologetically. Celebrate your unique path, knowing that living authentically not only enriches your life but also contributes to a world that values and celebrates the diversity of all minds.

Thank you for diving into this workbook and taking steps toward self-care, empowerment, and self-discovery. Your journey matters, and so does your voice. As someone navigating the world authentically as an Autistic adult, your insights can inspire and guide others who may be considering this workbook as a tool for their own growth.

If this workbook has provided you with helpful strategies, sparked new perspectives, or simply made you feel seen and supported, we would love for you to share your thoughts in a review on Amazon. Your feedback isn't just about helping us as the authors—it's about building a community where others can feel encouraged to embrace their authentic selves too.

By spreading the word, you're helping create a world that values and celebrates neurodiversity. Thank you for being part of this journey, for sharing your story, and for helping us continue to champion the beauty of every unique mind. Together, we're making a difference!

Thank you for diving into this workbook and taking steps toward self-care, empowerment, and self-discovery. Your journey matters, and so does your voice. As someone navigating the world authentically as an Autistic adult, your insights can inspire and guide others who may be considering this workbook as a tool for their own growth.

If this workbook has provided you with helpful strategies, sparked new perspectives, or simply made you feel seen and supported, we would love for you to share your thoughts in a review on Amazon. Your feedback isn't just about helping us as the authors—it's about building a community where others can feel encouraged to embrace their authentic selves too.

By leaving a review, you're helping create a world that values and celebrates neurodiversity. Thank you for being part of this journey, for sharing your story, and for helping us continue to champion the beauty of every unique mind. Together, we're making a difference!

ALSO BY NEURO NURTURE

Made in the USA
Las Vegas, NV
01 March 2025

18905817R00033